Discover German Shepherds

by Victoria Marcos

© 2014 by Victoria Marcos
ISBN: 978-1-62395-637-0
eISBN: 978-1-62395-642-4
ePib ISBN: 978-1-62395-643-1
Images licensed from Fotolia.com
All rights reserved.
No portion of this book may be reproduced without express permission of the publisher.
First Edition
Published in the United States by Xist Publishing
www.xistpublishing.com
PO Box 61593 Irvine, CA 92602

German Shepherds are working dogs. They were first used to herd sheep.

They protect and herd many different animals.

They want to have a purpose.

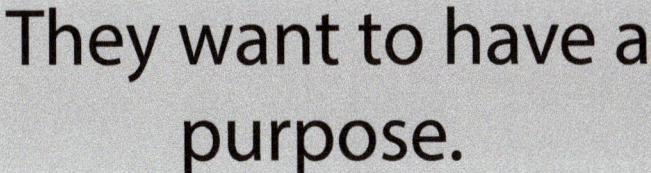

5

German Shepherds are very obedient and easy to train.

7

8

They are famous for their intelligence.

They learn tasks very quickly and obey correctly almost every time.

German Shepherds are used for search-and-rescue, police and military work.

They have an excellent sense of smell and aren't easily distracted from their work.

13

14

German Shepherds are also great swimmers.
They are very good at retrieving things from the water.

They are very active and energetic.

Although German Shepherds are strong, they can also be very gentle.

There was a time when almost all Seeing Eye dogs were German Shepherds.

Well-trained German Shepherds are very safe.

They are very protective of their families and territory.

They are especially protective of children.

German Shepherds are great companions.

They are both gentle and trustworthy.

As puppies they need to be around many different people, sights and sounds.

They can live peacefully with other pets if they are taught as puppies.

Sometimes German Shepherds get sick. A veterinarian can help when they don't feel good.

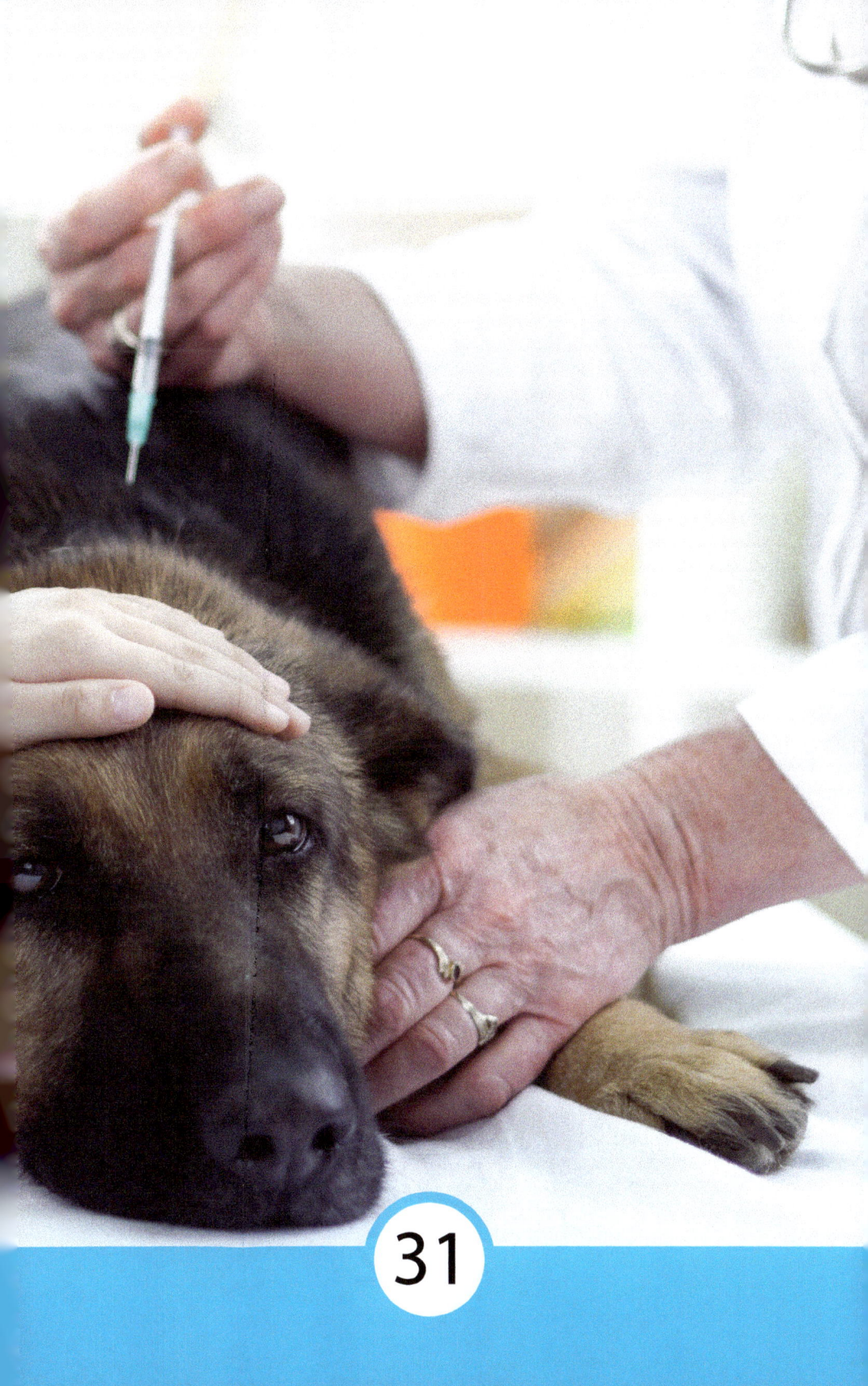

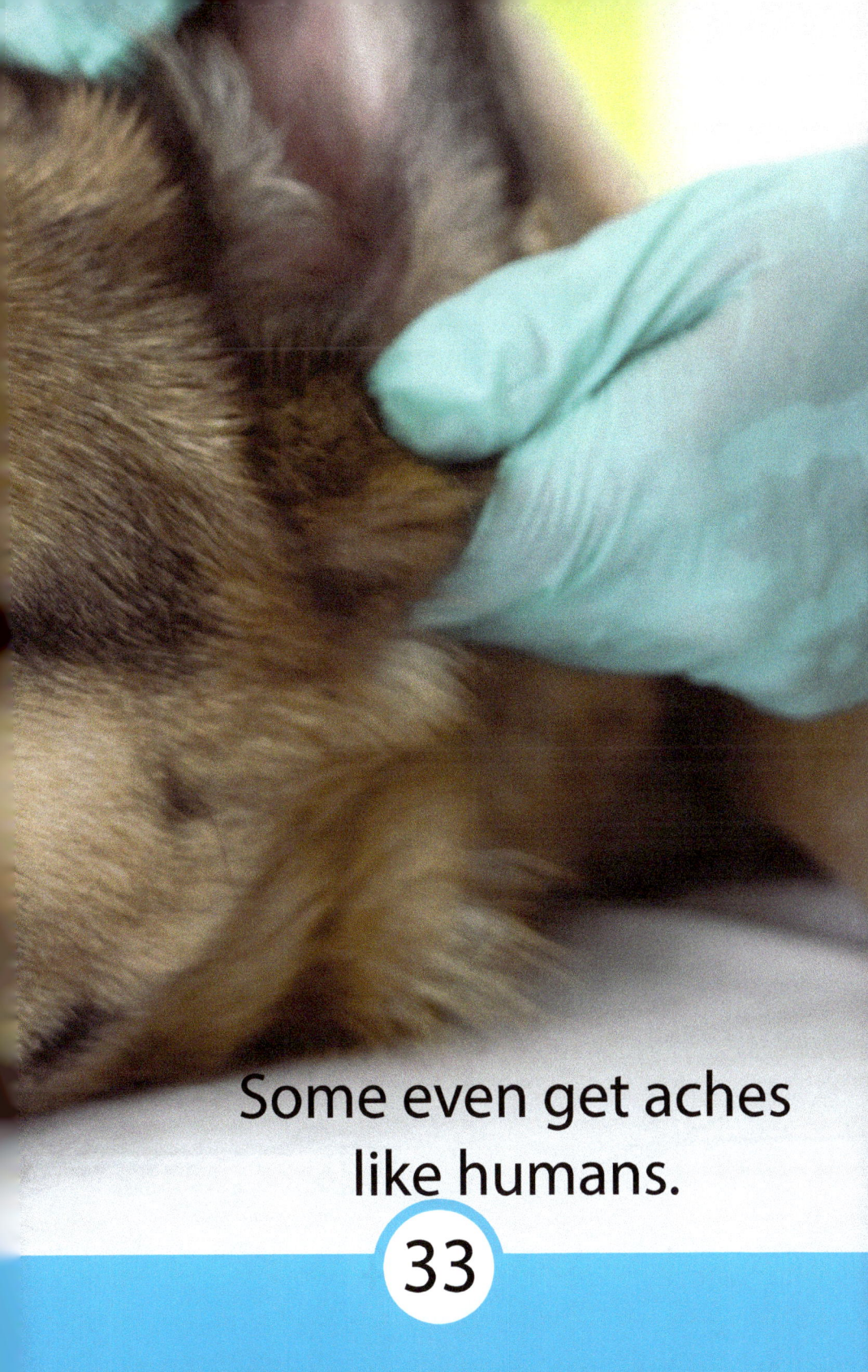

Some even get aches like humans.

German Shepherds make for great friends.

34

www.ingramcontent.com/pod-product-compliance
Ingram Content Group UK Ltd.
Pitfield, Milton Keynes, MK11 3LW, UK
UKHW021254180426
11947UKWH00010B/776